Revised Edition

Venus & Serena Williams

By Madeline Donaldson

AMAZING
ATHLETES

Lerner Publications Company/Minneapolis

Lerner Publications Company
A division of Lerner Publishing Group, Inc.
241 First Avenue North
Minneapolis, MN 55401 U.S.A.

Website address: www.lernerbooks.com

Library of Congress Cataloging-in-Publication Data

Donaldson, Madeline.
    Venus & Serena Williams / by Madeline Donaldson. — Rev. ed.
       p.   cm. — (Amazing athletes)
    Includes bibliographical references and index.
    ISBN-13: 978-0-8225-7595-5 (lib. bdg. : alk. paper)
    1. Williams, Venus, 1980– —Juvenile literature. 2. Williams, Serena, 1981– —Juvenile literature.
3. Tennis players—United States—Biography—Juvenile literature. I. Title. II. Title: Venus and Serena Williams.
GV994.A1D65 2008
796.3420922—dc22   2007005282

Manufactured in the United States of America
1 2 3 4 5 6 – DP – 13 12 11 10 09 08

TABLE OF CONTENTS

Serena reaches out to slam the ball over the net. She was battling Israeli teenager Shahar Peer in the 2007 **Australian Open**.

FIGHTING BACK

Serena Williams cracked another huge **return** to her opponent, Shahar Peer. They were playing in the **quarterfinals** of the 2007 Australian Open. This is the first of four **Grand Slam** tennis events played every year.

No one expected Serena to get this far in the **tournament.** Ongoing knee problems had forced her to withdraw from many tournaments in 2006. Her talented sister Venus also had injuries that kept her out of tournaments in 2006. In fact, Venus withdrew from the 2007 Australian Open because of a wrist injury. But both are determined competitors. They don't give up.

Injuries have kept Venus off the court lately. But she's always ready to cheer on Serena from the sidelines.

Winning the first set, Shahar Peer pushed Serena to play her best tennis in the quarterfinals.

The quarterfinal against Peer tested Serena's will to win. Serena started slowly. She lost the first set, 6–3. But then she regained her confidence and won the second set, 6–2.

Coming into the tournament, Serena was ranked 81st in the world. Venus was ranked 48th.

At first, Serena seemed to have it easy in the final set. Then Peer thundered back to tie the set 4–4. Peer managed to get to **break point** three times in the next game. Each time, Serena belted a **serve** that Peer couldn't return. Serena went up 5–4. Then Peer tied the match 5–5 and even broke Serena's serve. The score was 5–6, against Serena.

Serena powers a backhand to Shahar. Serena won the second set easily. But she had to work hard in the third set.

In the twelfth game, Serena dug deeply to even the score at 6–6. Then she let her power rip. She smashed through the next two games and won the set 8–6. She'd reached the **semifinal!**

After the win, Serena shakes hands with Shahar. Their match took almost three hours.

Serena went on to win her semifinal match. This brought her to the first Grand Slam **final** of 2007. She played the world's number-one player, Maria Sharapova. Serena again showed her outstanding ability. She tore through the match in about an hour, winning 6–1, 6–2. Afterward, Serena said, "It was an awesome win. . . . Tell me no, and I'll show you I can do it."

Serena strikes a fun pose as she holds up her Australian Open singles trophy.

Venus *(left)* and Serena *(right)* started playing tennis when they were very young. Their father, Richard, was their first coach.

Growing Up

Venus and Serena Williams grew up in Compton, a town in southern California. They were the youngest of five daughters. Their dad, Richard, had caught the tennis bug. He had been teaching their older sisters to play tennis.

In 1984, when Venus was four, she started hitting tennis balls with her family. A year later, when Serena turned four, she also picked up a racket for the first time. Before long, it was clear the two girls had a lot of natural talent. Their early skills amazed Richard and the girls' mother, Oracene. (Richard and Oracene divorced in 2003.)

Walls in the ghettos of Los Angeles often were covered with graffiti.

The Williamses' neighborhood was in the **ghetto.** This part of Compton had high crime rates. Gang violence was common. The neighborhood's tennis courts weren't in great shape. The Williams sisters had to be careful when they practiced. Sometimes fights broke out between the gangs near the courts, and the girls would have to leave. But the danger didn't stop them from going to the courts nearly every day.

Richard wanted his daughters to be great tennis players. But he also wanted them to do well in school. He told Venus and Serena they couldn't play tennis if they hadn't done their homework. Both sisters worked hard at tennis and in school.

Over time, gang members came to respect what Richard and his daughters were doing on Compton's cracked courts. The gangs left them alone.

On Compton's courts, Richard pushes Venus in a ball-filled shopping cart.

Venus's tennis skills wowed a lot of professional coaches.

TURNING PROFESSIONAL

Venus was the older sister by a little over a year. At age nine, she began playing in and winning junior tennis tournaments. At the same time, Serena was also winning tournaments. They got a lot of attention when they played. The attention made it hard for them to focus on schoolwork. Richard decided Venus and Serena should stop playing junior tournaments.

The girls kept practicing, though. With their dad coaching them, they got better and better. They improved in both **singles** (when one person plays another) and **doubles** (when two two-person teams play). After many months, Richard felt he'd done what he could. His daughters needed a better coach.

Rick Macci, a tennis coach from Florida, flew to California. He couldn't believe how good the girls were. He called Venus a "female Michael Jordan." Coaching cost a lot of money. Rick offered to coach the girls for free. But the family would have to move to Florida. Venus and Serena's parents talked it over. They decided to quit their jobs and move the entire family to Florida.

Rick Macci (left) coached Venus (below) and Serena from 1991 to 1995.

Venus and Serena practiced many hours each day. They got stronger. They gained more experience in singles and doubles. Instead of going to school, the girls were taught at home. Richard and Oracene were still very serious about education. They wanted their children to be smart people, not just smart tennis players.

In 1994, Venus started bugging her parents about turning **professional.** Even though she was only fourteen, Venus wanted her chance to play against the best women players. Her parents finally agreed. But she could only play in a certain number of tournaments a year. They put the same limits on Serena when she turned pro in 1995.

In October 1994, Venus played her first match as a professional. She won!

Companies approached the Williamses with offers of money if the girls would **endorse** (help sell) their products. The family signed contracts with companies that make sports equipment and clothing. The endorsement money helped pay for travel, housing, training partners, and other expenses.

Venus holds up tennis shoes made by Reebok. She first agreed to endorse Reebok products in 1995.

Serena *(between Richard and Venus)* is pretty quiet during an interview with reporters. Serena turned professional in 1995.

LIFE ON AND OFF THE COURT

Venus and Serena were playing some of the best players in the women's tennis tour. After a few years, the girls were ranked in the top 100 by the **Women's Tennis Association (WTA)**. This group ranks players based on how well they perform at tournaments.

School was still a huge priority. In 1997, Venus graduated from high school. This big step was paired with success on the court. She made it to her first Grand Slam final, the 1997 **U.S. Open.** She lost to Martina Hingis. Serena graduated in 1998. That year, the sisters played in the Australian Open. During the tournament, they had to play each other for the first time as professionals. Neither liked the experience much. "It wasn't funny, eliminating my little sister," Venus said after beating Serena.

Venus and Serena graduated from the Driftwood Academy in Florida. Both earned good grades.

For the next five years, Venus and Serena enjoyed lots of success. Serena was the first Williams sister to win a Grand Slam singles event. In 1999, she beat Hingis at the U.S. Open. Venus followed by winning Wimbledon in England in 2000. That same year, they took part in the Summer Olympic Games in Australia. They each took home a gold medal for their doubles play. Venus won a gold in singles.

Venus and Serena proudly show off their gold medals from the 2000 Olympics.

The last time any sisters played one another in a Grand Slam final was in 1884!

In 2001, the Williams sisters played each other for the first time in a Grand Slam final. The U.S. Open was on television at night. Huge lights lit up **Center Court**. A choir performed music. Fireworks went off. Celebrities were on hand in the stands. Perhaps the pressure got to the sisters. Neither played her best tennis. Venus beat Serena in two sets.

By 2002, the sisters were more used to playing one another. They reached the finals of the French Open, Wimbledon, and the U.S. Open. Serena won all three events. She was ranked number one in the world. Venus nailed the number two spot.

The sisters hug each other after the 2002 French Open final. Serena won the match, 7–5, 6–3.

In January 2003, they again faced each other in the Australian Open final. Serena won in a tough battle. Her win meant she was the champion of all four Grand Slam events! The sisters also won the Australian doubles championship. Serena followed up this win by defeating Venus at Wimbledon.

Venus and Serena hold up the trophy for winning the doubles final at the Australian Open. Serena would later gain the singles title against Venus in a three-set match.

Despite the success, the Williams family suffered a blow in September 2003. Yetunde Price, their older sister, was murdered in Compton. Then, in 2004, injuries plagued both tennis stars. Serena lost in the Wimbledon final. Venus had a hard time getting to the finals of any tournament. But she bounced back in 2005, winning Wimbledon. Serena won her second Australian Open title that year.

Excited and happy, Venus holds up her 2005 Wimbledon trophy. She beat Lindsay Davenport in the final.

Meanwhile, the sisters showed fans their fashion talents. They began designing their own tennis outfits. Venus also started V Starr Interiors, her own interior design firm in Florida. Serena formed her own clothing line, Aneres. Her designs can be found in shops in Florida and California. They also have been on television. "Venus & Serena: For Real" appeared on the ABC Family Channel. Ongoing injuries kept both sisters off the court for most of 2006. Neither got past the quarterfinals in any Grand Slam. Many doubted their commitment to tennis. Writers said they didn't play enough tournaments to regain their rankings. Others suggested they needed to play more often to avoid getting more injuries.

Aneres, the name of Serena's clothing line, is Serena spelled backward.

Serena cracks a backhand to Maria Sharapova during the 2007 Australian Open final. Serena easily won, 6–1, 6–2.

As the Grand Slam events started in 2007, fans wondered what to expect. Both sisters showed up for the Australian Open. But Venus withdrew with a wrist injury. Serena kept winning, with several hard-fought matches. The hardest was her nearly three-hour quarterfinal against Israeli teenager, Shahar Peer. Serena fought a tight semifinal before blowing away Sharapova in the final. Next comes the French Open in May. Serena claims, "I'm ready to start training . . . already."

Selected Career Highlights

Venus's Career Highlights

2007 Withdrew from Australian Open with a wrist injury
As of April, ranked number 29 on the WTA Tour

2006 Injuries limited her play throughout the year
Ended the year ranked number 46 on the WTA Tour

2005 Won her third Wimbledon singles title
Ended the year ranked number 10 on the WTA Tour

2004 Performed poorly at Grand Slam events, reaching the
quarterfinals only of French Open
Ended the year ranked number 9 on the WTA Tour

2003 Reached singles final of the Australian Open for the first time but
lost to Serena
Reached singles final of Wimbledon but lost to Serena
Ended the year ranked number 11 on the WTA Tour

2003 Reached singles final of the Australian Open for the first time

2002 Reached number 1 ranking for the first time
Ended the year ranked number 2 (after Serena)

2001 Won singles titles at two Grand Slam events (Wimbledon and the
U.S. Open, when she beat Serena) and four other tour events
Ended the year ranked number 3 on the WTA Tour

2000 Won singles titles at two Grand Slam events (Wimbledon and
the U.S. Open) and at three other tour events
Won the singles gold medal at the Olympic Games in Sydney,
Australia
Ended year ranked number 3 on the WTA Tour

1999 Won singles titles at six tour events
Ended the year ranked number 3 on the WTA Tour

1998 Won singles titles at three tour events
Beat Serena in their first professional matchup in the opening
round of the Australian Open
Ended the year ranked number 5 on the WTA Tour

1997 First woman since 1978 to reach the finals at her first
U.S. Open appearance
Ended the year ranked number 22 on the WTA Tour

Serena's Career Highlights

2007 Won her third singles title at the Australian Open
As of April, ranked number 11 on the WTA Tour

2006 Injuries forced her out of most tournaments,
including Wimbledon and the French Open
Ended the year ranked number 95 on the WTA Tour

2005 Won her second singles title at the Australian Open
Ended the year ranked number 11 on the WTA
Tour

2004 Injuries kept her off the court most of the year
Reached the singles final of Wimbledon but lost
to Maria Sharapova
Ended the year ranked number 7 on the WTA Tour

2003 Won singles title at the Australian Open for the first time
Successfully defended her 2002 Wimbledon singles title by
defeating Venus
Along with Grand Slam wins from 2002, held titles in all four Grand
Slam events
Ended the year ranked number 3 on the WTA Tour

2003 Won singles title at the Australian Open for the first time
Along with Grand Slam wins from 2002, held titles in all four events

2002 Won singles titles at three Grand Slam events (the French Open,
Wimbledon, and the U.S. Open), all against Venus
Reached number 1 ranking for the first time (replacing Venus).
Ended year ranked number 1
Named Female Athlete of the Year by the *Associated Press*

2001 Won singles titles at two tour events
Ended the year ranked number 6 on the WTA Tour

2000 Won singles titles at three tour events
Ended the year ranked number 6 on the WTA Tour

1999 Won singles titles at one Grand Slam event (U.S. Open) and four
other tour events
Ended the year ranked number 4 on the WTA Tour

1998 Ended the year ranked number 20 on the WTA Tour

1997 Entered the WTA Tour ranked number 453; three weeks later, she
was ranked 102. Ended the year ranked 99

Glossary

Australian Open: the Australian Grand Slam event played every January

break point: when the player receiving the serve can win the game by scoring the next point. If the receiver scores the point against the server, the serve is said to be broken.

Center Court: at a tennis stadium, the main court, surrounded by the best seats, where the most important matches are played

doubles: a tennis match in which two-person teams play each other

endorse: to help sell products by appearing in ads on television or in magazines. The company that makes the products pays money to the person endorsing the products.

final: the last match in a series of tennis matches. The winner of the final match claims the championship for that year.

ghetto: an area of a city in which a specific group of people live

Grand Slam: in tennis, the name given to four championships played around the world each year. The events are the Australian Open, the French Open, Wimbledon (in England), and the U.S. Open.

match: a tennis contest that is won when one player or team wins a specified number of games and sets

professional: being able to play in tournaments for money

quarterfinals: a round of a tournament that is two wins away from the final

return: the shot played by the player receiving the serve

semifinals: a round of a tournament that is one win away from the final

serve: a hit of the tennis ball to start a tennis game

set: in a tennis match, a group of six or more games. A set must be won by at least two games or in a tiebreaker. Women's tennis matches have a maximum of three sets. The person who wins two of the sets wins the whole match. Winning two sets in a row is called winning in straight sets.

singles: a tennis match that pits one player against another

tennis tour: the yearly schedule, or circuit, of tennis tournaments held around the world. Professional players don't have to play in all the tournaments, but they must play in enough to keep up their tennis ranking.

tournament: a series of contests in which a number of people or teams take part, hoping to win the championship final

U.S. Open: The American Grand Slam event played every September in New York. Players from around the world compete to win the U.S. Open final in singles and doubles.

Women's Tennis Association (WTA): the governing body of professional women's tennis players. The WTA determines tennis rankings. The rankings show how well a player is playing compared to other players.

Further Reading & Websites

Armentrout, David, Armentrout, Patricia. *Venus & Serena Williams*. Vero Beach, FL: Rourke Publishing, 2005.

Bradley, Michael. *Serena Williams*. New York: Benchmark Books, 2005.

Sandler, Michael. *Tennis: Victory for Venus Williams*. New York: Bearport Publishing, 2006.

Storey, Rita. *Tennis*. London: Franklin Watts Ltd, 2007.

Vale, Mark. *Junior Tennis: A Complete Coaching Manual for the Young Tennis Player*. New York: Barrons Educational Series, 2006.

Watson, Galadriel Findley. *Venus and Serena William*. New York: Weigl Publishers, 2005.

Williams, Serena, and Venus Williams. *How to Play Tennis*. New York: DK Children, 2004.

Sony Ericsson WTA Tour
http://www.sonyericssonwtatour.com/1/
The official website of the Sony Ericsson WTA Tour has rankings, late-breaking news stories, biographies, photographs and more.

Sports Illustrated for Kids
http://sikids.com/
The Sports Illustrated for Kids website covers all sports, including tennis.

Venus and Serena Fan Website
http://www.venusandserena.homestead.com
This website provides fans with recent news stories, biographies, photographs, and more.

Index

Photo Acknowledgments

The images in this book are used with permission of: © Torsten Blackwood/AFP/Getty Images, p. 4; © Dylan Martinez/Reuters/CORBIS, p. 5; © Clive Brunskill/Getty Images, pp. 6, 7, 25; © Greg Wood/AFP/Getty Images, p. 8; © Quinn Rooney/Getty Images, p. 9; © Ken Levine/Getty Images, pp. 10, 13, 14, 16; © Joseph Sohm/ChromoSohm, Inc./CORBIS, p. 12; © Al Bello/Getty Images, pp. 17, 19; © Reuters/NewMedia Inc./CORBIS, p 18; © Gary M. Prior/Getty Images, pp. 21, 28; © Jamie Squire/Getty Images, p. 22; © Francois Guillot/AFP/Getty Images, p. 23; © Sean Garnsworthy/Getty Images, p. 24; © Ezra Shaw/Getty Images, p. 27; © Duomo/CORBIS, p. 29.

Cover: © Daniel Berehulak/Getty Images (left); © Scott McDermott/CORBIS (right)